Cooee!

A play by Katy Forde

Illustrated by Jeffrey Diamond

Characters

Kai

Kez

Snazz
(a green tree snake)

Kooka

(a kookaburra)

Bluey

(a satin bowerbird)

Poss

(a brushtail possum)

In the bush

Kooka: Coo, coo, coo! Ka, ka, ka!

Poss: Eeee!

Snazz: Why are you two making that terrible noise?

Kooka: There are children coming!

Snazz: Children?

Bluey: Oh, I hear them. I think they're crying.

Kez and Kai enter, crying loudly.

The animals surround the children.

Kai: *(screams)* A snake! Get away from me!

Snazz: How rude. I won't hurt you.

Poss: Why are you crying, children?

Kez: We're lost in the bush!

Kai: We're scared. We can't find our dad!

Bluey: We'll help you find your dad, but first, try to calm down. Take a deep breath in and out. There. Feel better?

Kez: Yes, thank you.

Snazz: Now, let's think. How can we find your dad?

Kai: We could shout the special word that Dad taught us.

Kez: Yes, Dad taught us a special word to shout if we get lost in the bush.

Poss: Great! What's the word?

Kai:
Kez: I can't remember!

Kooka: Oh dear.

They hear a chak-chak-chak sound.

Kez: It's a helicopter!

Kai: Maybe Dad is in that helicopter, looking for us.

Kez: I know! Let's write "HELP" in big letters on the ground. If Dad's in the helicopter, he'll see it and know we're here.

Poss: That's a great idea!

Snazz: What can we use to make the letters?

Bluey: We can use the blue things in my bower.

Kai: What's a bower?

Bluey: Look behind that tree.

Kez: Wow! It's like a tiny stage covered in blue – blue feathers, blue flowers and blue lids. It's beautiful.

Bluey: It's BLUE-tiful!

Kai: These blue things are so **little**. I don't think we can use them to make big letters.

Bluey: I only use **little** blue things to decorate my bower. Yesterday, I found that **big** blue thing over there, but it was too big to put in my bower.

Kez: Hold on! That big blue thing is a mobile phone!

Kai: Yay! I'll call Dad.

Kooka: I'm so happy, I could sing!

Bluey: Me too!

Snazz: Kooka and Bluey, please be quiet. Let them call their dad.

Kez: Yes, what are you waiting for, Kai? Call home!

Kai: Dad won't be at home. He'll be out looking for us.

Kez: Then call him on his mobile phone.

Kai: I would, but …

Kez: But what?

Kai: I can't remember his mobile number! Can **you** remember it?

Kez: Umm … no.

Kooka: Now I feel like crying.

Poss: Me too, Kooka.

Snazz: It's all right. I have an idea.

Bluey: Tell us, Snazz!

Kooka: Yes, tell us!

Poss: Please tell us!

Snazz: Many years ago, a man stepped on me. I got such a fright, I bit him. Well, I said sorry, and I told him that I'm not deadly. But he just turned to his friend and screamed, "Call triple zero!"

Kez: Great idea, Snazz! We should call triple zero.

Kai: We can't do that! You're only supposed to call triple zero when it's an emergency.

Kez: This **is** an emergency!

Kai: But we're not in any danger right now.

Kooka: That's true, you're not in any danger right **now**, but it gets very cold here at night doesn't it, Poss?

Poss: Yes, and you don't have a furry tail to keep you warm.

Kai: You're right. This **is** an emergency. I'll call triple zero.

Kai dials the number.

Kai: Oh no!

Bluey: What's wrong?

Kai: The phone is dead.

Kez: Oh no! What are we going to do?

Kai: I wish we could remember that special word that Dad taught us to call out, if we get lost in the bush.

Kooka: I wonder if it's anything like **my** special sounds. When I'm scared, I puff out my feathers and cry, COO, COO, COO! KA, KA, KA!

Poss: And I fluff out my fur and squawk, EEEE!

Kez: Wait, Kooka! Say the first part of your call again.

Kooka: You mean – COO!

Kez: Now you, Poss.

Poss: You mean – EEE!

Kez: Kai, are you thinking what I'm thinking?

Kai: I **think** I'm thinking what you're thinking!

Kez: I remember the special word Dad told us to shout if we're lost in the bush!

Kai: Me too! The animals helped us remember. Ready, Kez?

Kez: Ready, Kai!

Kai:
Kez: COOEE!

In the distance, Dad replies COOEE.

Kez: I think that's Dad! Let's call again!

Kai:
Kez: COOEE!

Again, Dad calls COOEE.

Kez: It **is** Dad! He will find us now.

Kai: Thank you, everyone! Thank you **so** much! You helped Dad find us.

Kooka: Now I feel like singing!

Poss:
Bluey: Me too!

Snazz: Yes, even **I** feel like singing right now.

Kai:
Kez: So let's sing!

The animals and the children sing a song.

ALL: *If you're out in the bush one day,*

And you find you've lost your way,

There's one word you need to say –

But SHOUT so they'll hear from far away:

COOEE!